The
Reduced History of
DOGS

First published in 2007 by
André Deutsch Ltd
An imprint of the
Carlton Publishing Group
www.carltonpublishing.co.uk

Copyright © André Deutsch Ltd 2007

A CIP catalogue record for this book is available from the
British Library

ISBN: 978-0-233-00204-0

Printed in Singapore

Commissioning Editor: Martin Corteel
Project Art Editor: Darren Jordan
Production: Lisa French

The Reduced History of DOGS

The story of man's best friend in 101 barking-mad episodes

Chas Newkey-Burden Illustrations by Tony Husband

ANDRE
DEUTSCH

Other titles in the Reduced History series

The Reduced History of Cats

The Reduced History of Sex

The Reduced History of Britain

The Reduced History of Football

The Reduced History of Cricket

The Reduced History of Golf

The Reduced History of Rugby

The Reduced History of Tennis

INTRODUCTION

Dogs are rather brilliant, aren't they? Well, that brilliance didn't just emerge out of the ether, you know. Dogs have a whole history just like we humans do. It's true: as the human race has walked down the road that is life, dogs have been faithfully at our sides. They might occasionally chase after a rabbit, cock their leg over our snotty neighbours' prize plant or even savagely bite a small child's face off, but we still love 'em.

The following pages lead you through the story of man's best friend, from the wolf-like ancestors that plodded the earth millions of years ago to the world's first cloned dog. In between, we unleash the truth about the brave role the dog has played in wars and in fighting crime. We put our paws together for famous dogs from literature, film and television. Also given a quick sniff are many other major moments of mutt magnitude, including the Dangerous Dogs Act, the first dog in space and so much more.

The Reduced History of Dogs is as fun, bouncy and lively as any puppy. So put it on your lap and enjoy.

HIS BARK IS WORSE THAN HIS BITE

From wolf to woof!

The early evolution of the dog

Around 40 million years ago, a new branch of meat-eating mammals arrived on the scene. They immediately lifted their legs and did a wee, demanded a walk, impatiently strained on their leashes, barked at some old-school postmen and chased some squirrels. Hallelujah, the day of the dog was here.

Actually, it would be more accurate to say that the weekend of the wolf was here because these creatures, distinguished by their four meat-eating teeth, were the forerunners of wolves, who were themselves the

forerunners of dogs.

Experts believe that the most distant of the dog's ancestors lived in North America and were known as the Hesperocyon, which is a rubbish name by any standards. Imagine shouting that at your dog down the local path. You'd be laughed out of town – and rightly so!

Although North America is considered the location for the most distant doggie relatives, some similar happenings were soon, erm, happening in Europe. Pretty soon, the fledgling fidos were spreading across the globe.

And they called it puppy love
The dog diaspora continues apace

In Eurasia at this point, a canine evolution was also underway. These early dogs enjoyed a good long walk, as their relatives do today. More so in fact – they were soon migrating across Asia, Europe and Africa and spreading some doggie love wherever they went!

It's not known whether the inhabitants of each continent were opposed to this canine influx. But it is tempting to speculate that right-wing newspapers warned that these creatures were set to drain the country of all their social security funds and corrupt their children. You can also imagine old-school bigots complaining: "Bleeding dog-ancestors, coming over here and stealing our bones."

These dog-ancestors evolved down the centuries in response to climate and habitat. They would also follow human beings around in the hope of being thrown a scrap of food. In return, they offered protection from vermin.

Dogs were tamed very quickly by human contact. Lo and behold, the greatest human–animal relationship in history was formed.

Hungry like the wolf
The day of the Dingo dawns

We've all been there: those days when you are so hungry you just can't stop eating. Well, Australian Dingoes go there every day: these wild dogs have been known to eat everything from lizards to small rodents and even sheep and kangaroos. That's one hell of a set menu!

Originally kept by Aboriginals as hunting companions, Dingoes – descended from the Indian wolf – have also been used as sentries and camp cleaners (as in dogs that clean camps, not dogs that clean with a limp paw).

Nowadays, Dingoes are found throughout south-east Asia and northern Australia. Owing to interbreeding with other dogs and also because the Dingo has only one breeding cycle per year, there are fears that Dingoes might become extinct in the future.

Greece lightning!
The dawn of hunting

The word for hunting in ancient Greek was *knegia*, which is derived from the word *kynos* meaning "dog". So which animal do you think the ancient Greeks used a lot for hunting? That's right – dogs! Honestly, you are clever.

Using a forerunner of the Greyhound called the Vertragus, the Greeks were indulging in a fledgling form of hare coursing many centuries before a load of posh toffs forced their way into the chamber of the House of Commons to protest at anti-hunting legislation.

Greek goddess Artemis once – according to legend – managed to fend off some unwanted interest from a man using dogs. Bathing naked in the woods, she found herself being stared at by some old perv called Actaeon. So she magically turned him into a stag and ordered his own dogs to rip him to pieces. Down boy, indeed!

5 Fido food!
People actually eat dogs!

Feeling peckish? You might not be by the end of this page. From the time of Confucius, Chinese people have eaten dog meat. Sorry to have just come out and said it, but there really is no way around it.

Interestingly, dog meat is not some cheap substitute for nicer meats – be honest, we've all stared at our late-night doner kebab and wondered. Instead, it is the most expensive meat choice in China.

So it is only an occasional meal for most Chinese people. Another occasional dog thing out there is the Chinese Year of the Dog, which comes around every 12 years. People born in the Chinese Year of the Dog are said to be loyal and honest. Famous dog people include Brigitte Bardot and Elvis Presley, both of whom feature later on in this book.

Returning to canine consumption, dog meat has also been popular at various times in other countries, including Cambodia, the Philippines, Switzerland and Indonesia. So if you find yourself in any of those countries being offered a meat you can't quite identify, the safest thing is to reply politely but firmly: "Nothing for me, thank you."

"Fancy a Chinese takeaway?"

Roman handlers
The canine melting-pot

If you are a dog lover then "a land of a thousand dogs" might sound like a rather jolly prospect. That is the name attributed to the Roman Empire, which was akin to a canine melting-pot where dogs served in a wide variety of roles.

Some Roman dogs were merely companions or guard dogs. However, others were used for a more brutal purpose. Huge Molossians – forerunners of the Mastiff breed – were used as attack dogs and sent directly into battle to kill and dismember the enemy. How ghastly! Beware of the dog on a huge scale! The Romans might have been the first to use Molossian dogs but, as we shall see imminently, they were not the last…

Hun-gry likes the wolf
Defending the realm

Attila the Hun attracted controversy galore as he strode around Europe invading countries and causing general havoc. Plenty of people therefore wanted to get to him and at the very least say "Steady on, old boy!" – or go even further and kill him.

Therefore, he needed to keep potential enemies away from his camp at night. He employed dogs to stand guard around his camp and warn him of any impending enemies. His favourite dogs were those old charmers the Molossians. Funny that, because later on Genghis Khan used the same dogs. These dogs were clearly the canine of choice for bloodthirsty conquerors!

8 Rescue me!
The search started here

"I know, let's train dogs to help us out."

The year is 980, the place is the Alps and a monastery and inn have just been built. Sounds great, huh? Mine's a pint of ale, thanks.

Trouble was, the monks who lived there found themselves frequently called out to find travellers who'd become lost or avalanched. They had a reasonable amount of success at this, but in time they decided they could do with an extra set of hands.

Or an extra set of paws, to be exact. The monks began to use guard dogs to keep watch on their dwellings and then decided to try and use the dogs to help find stranded people. The dogs proved to be a huge success and frequently helped the monks find people, even those covered in snow.

This is the official story of the advent of the rescue dog. As we shall see, some of it has been disputed. But the legend – if not the actual era – of the rescue dog started here. And nobody – apart from village drunks – would dispute that.

Best of breed: Bloodhounds
Smells like a keen spirit!

Can you smell something? No? Maybe it's just us. But if you had a Bloodhound at your feet he or she would be able to smell all sorts of things that your humble human hooter would fail to detect.

Bloodhounds have been used as tracking dogs since the Middle Ages and can sometimes detect a single human skin cell that has lain dormant for several days. In pre-Civil War America, they were used to track runaway slaves and they have continued to play a huge part in the history of the United States – most recently playing a starring role in the heroic search for survivors at Ground Zero after the World Trade Center attacks.

Bloodhounds' long, low-set ears serve to assist them in their sniffing: they stop the wind from blowing away whatever the Bloodhound is smelling.

Known as "gentle giants", Bloodhounds are among the friendliest of large dogs and are keen and loyal companions. Although they are difficult to obedience-train – their strong tracking instincts give them a slightly insubordinate streak – persistence always pays off. There is something special about Bloodhounds as they plod – and they definitely plod, rather than walk – alongside their owners. And these days, when prisoners seem to be able to just walk out of jails, Bloodhounds are needed more than ever!

10 A proper Charlie!
The king who loved dogs

Imagine you became king or queen of England. Imagine this happened in the olden days when monarchs had far more power than they do nowadays. All those possibilities: what would be the first thing you'd do?

That's right! Sit around and hang out with your dogs! At least, that's more or less what King Charles II did, if the diaries of Samuel Pepys are to be believed. Pepys, and other diarists of the time, claimed that Charles spent more time with his beloved Spaniels than he did on affairs of state.

His love of his dogs went so far that he issued a decree that the King Charles Spaniel breed could not be forbidden entrance into any public building, including the House of Commons.

Some might say that Charles was a little irresponsible paying so much attention to his dogs, compared to all the important stuff like taxes, foreign policy, the Great Fire of London and the great plague. But he was known as the "merry monarch" – which shows that he probably got the balance just about right.

A guiding paw!
The dogs that are our eyes and ears

Throughout these pages, you will read many tales of heroic behaviour from dogs. Few are as awesome as that of the guide dog. The first instance of a dog assisting the blind came in 1789 at a hospital in Paris. However, it isn't until the end of the First World War that the tale really begins. The German government began to train dogs to assist soldiers who had been blinded during the war. By 1930, both America and Britain had got in on the act.

The guide dog is now a worldwide phenomenon and they are allowed access to many places that other dogs are banned from. Recently, "hearing dogs" have also been trained to guide deaf people around.

Many thousands of people have seen their lives transformed by guide and hearing dogs. Bless every single dog that has helped out this way. Truly inspiring stuff.

"Find the Eiffel Tower, boy."

Dogging fashions
From conquistadors to Collymore!

When Spanish conquistadors arrived in the Americas, they found a number of ways to scare the wits out of the natives who stood in their way, and one of their favourites involved our four-legged friends. They were already using dogs in their armies when some of the cruellest among the conquistador leaders hit upon the idea of getting their dogs to publicly execute native Americans. This activity was known as dogging.

Many, many years on – many centuries on, in fact – another sinister activity was given the same name. This time, it involved people who wandered around car parks watching other people having sex. Former footballer Stan Collymore was among the supporters of this activity. Whether it is bloodthirsty conquistadors or former footballers, you can't help but conclude that nobody comes out of the whole dogging business with much dignity intact.

Sadly, not all of the conquistadors' dogs survived intact at all. When Panfilo de Narvaez and his crew arrived in Florida, they faced tough resistance from the natives and were forced, through starvation, to eat their own dogs.

Fine and Dandie!

The fictional dogs who came true

Dandie Dinmont is a reasonably unremarkable character in Sir Walter Scott's novel *Guy Mannering*, which was published in 1815. "So what?" we hear you cry. "That book is soooo two centuries ago and this Dinmont character sounds, like, totally boring!"

Wait! There is a point to all this. Mr Dinmont owned a number of terriers and a whole breed of dogs was named after these terriers! See, you're interested now, aren't you?

With their lovely little legs and distinctive fluffy knot of hair on top of their heads, Dandie Dinmont Terriers are cuddly little terrors that come in two colours, pepper and mustard. Sixty years after *Guy Mannering* was published, during a meeting on the Scottish borders, the Dandie Dinmont Terrier Club was formed and this is now one of the oldest pedigree clubs on the entire planet.

So you see how important Mr Dinmont was in the history of dogs. Bet you feel pretty darn stupid for doubting us during that opening sentence!

14 Holy cow!
The Australian cattle dog

A position has arisen at farms across Australia for a dog that is willing to work all day in the blistering heat herding sheep and cows around. You will need to be able to withstand intense hardships and be totally confident when ordering around animals several times bigger than you. The ideal candidate will be the result of six decades of cross-breeding involving the Dingo, the Blue Merle Smooth Highland Collie, the Dalmatian and the Bull Terrier. Flaming galahs need not apply.

WANTED
CATTLE
DOGS
GOOD RATE
OF PAY

"Don't worry, they'll ban this one day."

In 1836, the first Waterloo Cup was contested. No, it wasn't some sort of dog race to catch the last train at Waterloo station. Drunken commuters run that sort of race most nights of the week. Instead, the Waterloo Cup was run at Great Altcar in Merseyside and was a key fixture on the hare-coursing calendar.

Two Greyhounds would chase a live hare and once they caught it, the poor little hare wouldn't stand a chance. Not ideal for the hare.

Naturally, therefore, the event became hugely controversial and the Hunting Act 2004 meant that there was no Waterloo Cup in 2006. Supporters of the Cup vowed that they would return in the future. You can't help thinking that a nation of hares will be praying that there is never another Waterloo Cup.

Boxing clever
The dog on the tuckerbox

Should you ever find yourself sightseeing in the Snake Gully area of Australia (it's about five miles outside Gundagai in New South Wales – you can't miss it) then make sure you don't miss the dog on the tuckerbox statue.

This monument was erected in 1926, but was not directly paying tribute to a dog. It was actually inspired by a poem written by one of Australia's early pioneers, which outlines how a dog guarded the tuckerbox – the food supply of the pioneers – as they went about their work. A wishing well was placed in front of the statue, the proceeds of which went to a local hospital.

Nowadays, there is a series of eateries in the area, including a KFC and a Subway restaurant. The dog that inspired the poem showed great restraint not eating the contents of the tuckerbox; you can't help wondering whether he'd have been so strong at resisting the pull of a KFC!

17 Pet cemetery

Greyfriars Bobby and his decade-long mourning

Surely we are all agreed that, compared to dogs, cats are a bit rubbish. For a start, four-legged felines have little sense of loyalty when compared to dogs, who are loyal to a fault. And has there ever been a more loyal dog than Greyfriars Bobby?

Bobby was a Skye Terrier owned by policeman John Gray in Edinburgh in the nineteenth century. When Mr Gray died in 1858, he was buried in Greyfriars Kirkyard and Bobby spent the remaining 10 years of his own life sitting on his master's grave.

The Lord Provost of Edinburgh even paid for Bobby's licence renewal, making him the responsibility of the city council, thus saving the un-owned Bobby from being put down. When Bobby eventually passed away, he was buried inside Greyfriars Kirkyard, near his owner's grave.

Many dog owners have mourned the loss of a beloved pet. But how many of us can say we mourned with such sincerity as dear Bobby did? Today a statue of Bobby – who is now the subject of a movie – stands proudly outside a nearby pub. We all lift our glasses to him.

18 A home from home
Battersea Dogs' Home is born

How much is that doggie in the window?* No, not that one, that one!
No! Not him, her! This is the sort of insane and frustrating conversation
that must go on any time a child is taken within a mile of Battersea Dogs'
Home. All the same, given the superb work that the home has done for
the last 140 years, we reckon you shouldn't get too worked up about it.

From its origins in 1860 in Holloway, north London, to the present
day, the home has produced more happy endings than a seedy masseur.
Throughout the year, the home takes in unwanted and stray dogs, looks
after them and sells them to families that do want them and are capable
of looking after them. It's as simple and wonderful as that.

No wonder the BBC has produced some entertaining and moving
documentaries set in Battersea Dogs' Home. Just sit still for
a moment and think about all those unwanted dogs
being taken in and then given to loving families.
Go on, think about it. Crying yet? Of course you
are, you'd need a heart of stone not to.

* In answer to this question, doggies cost £70 at Battersea Dogs' Home.

LET THE DOG SEE THE RABBIT

19 Breeding heaven!
The Kennel Club is formed

In April 1873, a group of people met up in a flat in England. Big deal, you might think. Well it was, because that meeting led to the establishment of the first Kennel Club. Within a year, the club had published a stud book. No, this wasn't a hard-backed gay porn annual, instead it was a list of pedigrees of dogs. The bible of bone-eaters, you might think. Actually, that sounds a bit lewd, too. But you get the idea. It became the book that influenced dog-breeders for the rest of time.

Kennel Clubs soon followed around the world – the French in 1882 and the American in 1883 – and were soon busying themselves with the breeding and showing of pedigree dogs.

If you want to create a new breed or pedigree, you won't get anywhere without the approval of your nation's Kennel Club. Go on, just you try. You will fail and everyone will laugh their heads off at you.

"I'd never want to join a club that would have me as a member."

20 The wrestling dogs!

Tosas do it the sumo way

Two fat blokes, wearing nappies and wrestling in a small ring: what sort of person would enjoy that as a spectacle? Well, as we all know, sumo wrestling has become a hugely successful sport since its inception 1,500 years ago. The Tosa breed, of Japanese origin, is also known to many as the sumo dog. This is because sumo wrestling is the basis for the traditional Japanese dog fight.

It is hard to imagine why a Tosa dog would want to get involved in such a dog fight. After all, the prize is a cloth apron. A cloth apron. Has there even been a more rubbish prize in the history of sport? Even football's Carling Cup seems exciting in comparison.

The Tosa is banned from many countries and some believe this is because of its size and violent background. We reckon this ban was brought in to avoid the Tosa boring other dogs to tears by bringing out its collection of aprons and blabbering on about its various successes.

Grub's up!
The dawn of commercial dog food

We've all seen that look of sheer joy that comes over a dog's face when you spoon its food into its bowl. Well we – and the dogs – have a man from Ohio called James Spratt to thank for all this joy. In 1860, Mr Spratt was on a work trip to England when he saw a group of dogs being fed biscuits left over by sailors. He felt he could offer them more exciting nosh and came up with a meal that combined wheatmeal, vegetables, beetroot and meat.

His combination became popular among country gents in England and his operation soon expanded to the US. Before long, a pet food industry began to thrive, with horsemeat and dry biscuits also on the menu.

During the Depression in the 1930s, owners adopted cheaper ways of feeding their dogs, with cereal and grain meals becoming more popular than the more expensive raw meat. Nowadays, the choice is wider than ever with canned meat, dry biscuits, "soft-moist" varieties and – of course – endless dog treats on offer at every supermarket, pet shop and vets. Dogs today, eh? Spoilt rotten. Don't know they're born.

"Voilà!"

22 Best of breed: the Bulldog

This dog don't take no bull

Come and 'ave a go if you fink you're 'ard enuf! That is the sort of chant that most people would associate with the Bulldog. Well, most people are wrong. Perhaps in the early 1800s, when Bulldogs were used for bull baiting, it is true that they were somewhat on the aggressive side. But once bull baiting was banned in Great Britain in the 1830s, the Bulldog nearly died out altogether. However, they survived and most of their aggressive tendencies were bred out of them.

The modern-day Bulldog has a lovely personality and is a perfect pet for any family. However, although they are now friendly and playful, they are also very stubborn and protective. So don't mess with the best because the best don't mess.

They are so tenacious by nature that the Bulldog has come to be used as the mascot for a number of organizations, including armies and universities. And, lest we forget, the Bulldog is the symbol of Great Britain. Jolly good show.

23 Hurrying Huskies!
The dawn of the Iditarod race

Controversy-lovers listen in, it's time for another contentious entry. The Iditarod race is an annual dog sled competition in Alaska which started in the 1800s and continues to this day. The course is over 1,000 miles and teams of mushers (the people) and Siberian Huskies (that'll be the dogs) race along this course in sub-zero, gale-force conditions.

Sounds like fun, right? Maybe for the humans, but maybe not for the dogs. Animal rights groups have slammed the event as an exercise in cruelty and thrown all manner of contentious allegations at the event organizers. What is known is that each team's set of dogs – which will comprise between 12 and 16 animals – are carefully monitored by vets throughout the competition.

The arguments about the Iditarod continue to rage. However, the major source of contention about the event surely must be its name. What sort of idiot would call an event the Iditarod?

24 Nipper stands proud
The HMV dog

Aren't record shops brilliant? You give them money and in return they give you loads of music by artists that you enjoy. It's a genius concept and one that seems to suit everyone. But have you ever wondered how HMV came across their logo with the dog and the gramophone record? You have? Well, wonder no longer, for you are about to get the answer.

Nipper was a dog born in Bristol in 1884. He was part Bull Terrier, part Fox Terrier. His second owner, Francis Barraud, noticed that Nipper was fascinated by his record player and would wonder where the sound was coming from. One day, his owner painted a picture of Nipper standing curiously by the record player.

Barraud tried to sell the painting to several companies and magazines, but none of them bit until he knocked on the door of the Gramophone Company, who snapped it up. The painting eventually became the symbol of the HMV record stores.

Fame never went to Nipper's head. He continued his favourite pastimes of scrapping with other dogs and chasing rats. He is buried in Kingston-upon-Thames.

25 Putting on a show!

Cruft's is launched!

In 1886, a man called Charles who worked for a dog biscuit manufacturer held the First Great Terrier Show. "So what?" you may ask. "Why are you bothering us with that sort of information?" Because, you hasty buffoons, the man called Charles's surname was Cruft!

Still not worked it out? OK, that 1886 show was the forerunner for Cruft's, the annual four-day dog show that now draws over 140,000 visitors to its doors! See? There was a point to our little story, after all!

Nowadays, more than 24,000 dogs from hundreds of breeds and countries all over the world compete in the various categories. The Best of Breed and Best Puppy are the most prestigious categories.

There is now also another show called Scrufft's, where cross-breed dogs can compete. See, the dog world doesn't go for the sort of snobbery and elitism that you see in human talent shows like *Pop Idol* and *The X Factor*. The dog world lets any old mutt have a chance!

26 You're nicked!

The police dog era arrives

During the nineteenth century it was not unheard of for British police officers to take their pet dogs out on patrol with them. During the 1890s, Topper, a Fox Terrier, joined the Hyde Park police station and became the first full-time police dog. Forget Dixon of Dock Green, this was Topper of Hyde Park. Or Dixon of Dog Green, perhaps. (Perhaps not – Ed.) However, it was not until the 1920s that an experimental school was set up to train dogs for police work.

Then, after the Second World War, on the very first night of police and dog patrols in Hyde

Park, a dog foiled an attempted purse-snatch. As police dogs became a regular feature in the park, crime figures in the area plummeted. Before long, a specialized training unit was set up and the age of the police dog was well and truly here. The role of the police dog has developed alongside technology. Police often attach cameras to dogs' heads, so they can enter dangerous places and send footage back to the police.

Dogs might well be a man's best friend, but time after time they have proved to be a crook's worst enemy.

27 What a save!
A St Bernard saves Manchester United

Manchester United may not be a very canine football club on the surface (that honour would belong to Wolves, Blackburn Rovers and, erm, Liverpoodle) but were it not for a St Bernard dog, the club might have long ago disappeared altogether.

In 1902, the club – then known as Newton Heath, rubbish name, eh? – was on the verge of going under when it decided to hold a four-day bazaar to raise cash. One of the attractions at the bazaar was a St Bernard.

However, the little rascal escaped and during the search for it team captain Harry Stafford bumped into local businessman John Henry Davies, who became club president and saved the club!

A lovely little story, but let's have some fun here. Had it not been for that meeting in 1902, Old Trafford would never have witnessed the mercurial skills of Denis Paw, Bark Hughes, Woof Rooney and Cristiano Ronaldog. (Those last two are unacceptably bad. And you left out Nicky Mutt – Ed.)

Messing about on the river!

Montmorency joins three men in a boat

They say two's company and three's a crowd, but three men and a dog is a comedy tale – especially when they are on a boating holiday. Published in 1889, *Three Men in a Boat – To Say Nothing of the Dog* is one of English literature's funniest moments. Jerome K. Jerome's book sees three men take a hilariously disastrous journey down the River Thames, accompanied by Montmorency, a Fox Terrier.

Before the river trip has even begun, Montmorency has killed a dozen chickens, been dragged out of 114 street fights, been accused of murdering a cat and also confined a terrified neighbour to his tool-shed.

But once the three men set sail, Montmorency continues to amuse and entertain. He starts fights, sings, contributes a water rat to the Irish stew the men make and even joins in with the toast that the three men raise at the end of the story.

Three Men in a Boat is a moment of true comic genius in the history of literature. What was that? You think the author of *The Reduced History of Dogs* is worthy of being mentioned in the same breath as Jerome? Why, you are too kind.

It is no surprise at all that the tale of a boy who never grows up should feature a dog so prominently – dogs are a connection to the little child inside all of us.

The character of Peter Pan first appeared in 1902 in a book called *The Little White Bird*, but it is a dog not a bird that captured most hearts in the story. Nana the St Bernard dog was a popular character as the tale made the journey from an early-twentieth-century book to a legendary global narrative.

When the story was adapted for the big screen in 2003, Nana was played by a male St Bernard who even turned up to the première, complete with a white bonnet. What a star!

Best of breed: Chow Chows

It growls but it's not a bear

If an alien beamed down from outer space and saw a Chow Chow, it would probably think it was an overstuffed teddy bear rather than a dog. Actually, an alien probably wouldn't know what a teddy bear looked like. So if it saw a Chow Chow, it probably wouldn't know what it was.

Anyway, we're here to tell you that Chow Chows are dogs – and that's official, folks. They definitely aren't teddy bears. Trust us, we've looked into this. One of the oldest breeds on the block, the Chow Chow came from China but the date of its exact origins is unknown. It first arrived in Britain in 1780 and was originally used for herding, hunting and guarding.

Since it became a pet, the Chow Chow has become a popular companion. It is very much a one-person dog and has been known to snap at or bite anyone that gets on its tits. So don't mention its similarity to a teddy bear within earshot of one, nor its rather sissy little paws.

Chow Chows have a decent life-expectancy, sometimes living for over 15 years. Protect your own life-expectancy by showing a bit of respect to these dogs should you ever come across one.

The wild rover

He's all white, Jack!

We've all been suddenly thrown into traumatic and testing situations. Getting stuck in lifts, being forced to look at other people's holiday photographs or having to give stubbly Auntie Mildred a kiss at Christmas. Though these situations test us, we adapt and cope.

Which is what Buck, the hero of Jack London's novel *The Call of the Wild*, does when he is forced to leave his domestic comfort and work as a sled dog. Though he is surrounded by brutality and cruelty, he learns to cope and inspires all readers.

Go and buy a copy of *The Call of the Wild* and hold a mirror up to its pages. * You'll be able to read another of London's novels in the reflection. Well, kind of. What we're trying to say is that his book *White Fang* had a theme that was opposite to that of *The Call of the Wild*. In *White Fang*, a wild dog becomes civilized. This dog thus makes the opposite journey to Buck's.

Is that clear?

* Please don't actually do this. We don't mean to be taken literally. We are just trying to sound literary and clever.

"Fang, it's the wild for you!"

Dogs of war
The wonders of World War One

THE
UNKNOWN
DOG

Of all the tales of canine bravery to be related in these pages, the tales of the dogs during the First World War are particularly moving. Take the case of Airedale Jack, for instance. A stray, living in Battersea Dogs' Home, Jack was sent to war and saved an entire British battalion in France. The Germans had the British surrounded and the only hope for the Brits was to get word back to camp. Jack was sent with a message attached to his collar. He was hit several times by German fire, taking blows that smashed his jaw, ripped his body open and injured his paw. But he bravely soldiered on and delivered the message to HQ, whereupon he dropped dead. He saved the lives of the whole battalion.

This is just one instance of numerous accounts of dogs saving countless human lives during the First World War. Mercy dogs would find and retrieve wounded soldiers, sentry dogs would give silent warning of impending danger, mascot dogs would offer support and companionship to US soldiers. As so often happens in life, during some of the darkest hours in human history, dogs rose to the occasion. Go on, have a little weep if you want to.

Heart of class
Gonna make you a star

When you travel abroad, you might bring any number of things home with you: postcards, a local delicacy or some cheap fags. However, when film-making couple Larry Trimble and Jane Murfin travelled from Hollywood to Germany in the 1920s, they returned to the US with a dog.

And not just any dog. Originally – and rather comically – named Etzel von Oringer, Strongheart the German Shepherd became a worldwide superstar. Appearing in a host of movies, including an adaptation of *White Fang*, Strongheart boosted the popularity of German Shepherds around the world.

Tragically, while filming a movie in 1929, Strongheart fell against a hot studio light and was burned. The burn turned into a tumour and Strongheart died. Together with his mate, Strongheart produced a fair amount of offspring in his time, descendants of which live this very day.

Superstar Shepherd

How Rin Tin Tin conquered Hollywoof!

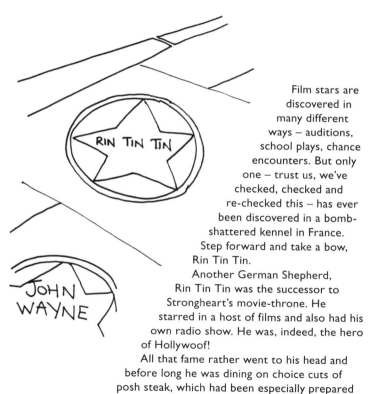

Film stars are discovered in many different ways – auditions, school plays, chance encounters. But only one – trust us, we've checked, checked and re-checked this – has ever been discovered in a bomb-shattered kennel in France. Step forward and take a bow, Rin Tin Tin.

Another German Shepherd, Rin Tin Tin was the successor to Strongheart's movie-throne. He starred in a host of films and also had his own radio show. He was, indeed, the hero of Hollywoof!

All that fame rather went to his head and before long he was dining on choice cuts of posh steak, which had been especially prepared for him by his private chef. He also got a star on the Hollywood Walk of Fame. When Rin Tin Tin died in 1932, he was returned to France for a ceremonial burial in a pet cemetery in Paris. Ooh, get him.

35 Kipling's canine
Rudyard writes *Thy Servant a Dog*

World-famous author seeks a servant. Must be content to sit comfortably on my knee, be willing to have his nose rubbed in any mess he makes and keep any chewing of my shoes to a minimum. In return, I will give him much love and feature him in my next book, *Thy Servant A Dog*. Please apply to Rudyard Kipling.

The White City whizzer

Mick the Miller outpaces 'em all

We've all seen very fast things occur in the world of sport. Arsenal and France's Thierry Henry positively burns towards goal, fans gallop towards the bar at half-time at any football match and the speed with which burgers sold outside any sporting event reappear back out of your mouth is incredible.

Well, an early Speedy Gonzalez in the world of sport was Mick the Miller – the first great Greyhound to race on English soil. Mick was brought over from Ireland in the late 1920s and raced at the White City stadium in London.

He set record after record and won many races, claiming victory in the English Derby on two occasions.

A spirited little fella, he was full of character and fun and made Greyhound racing the popular sport it is today virtually single-pawed. After his death, Mick was stuffed and is now displayed at the Walter Rothschild Zoological Museum in Tring. Rush over there and have a look!

37 Tintin time
The comic strip dog

OK, ladies, what is the most romantic thing a man has ever done for you? Has he ever named a character in one of his books after you? He hasn't? He isn't even an author, he's a gravedigger? Right, well imagine if your man did name a character in a book after you. You'd be pleased, right?

Then, imagine how Hergé's first girlfriend felt when she found out that he had named a character in the Tintin series after her. Pretty cheesed off, in all likelihood. The character was a dog!

Originally called Milou (after Hergé's ex), the dog's name became Snowy in the English version. A white Fox Terrier, Snowy was a faithful and fun companion to Tintin throughout all the comic books in the series. So what was Snowy like? Well, he loves drinking whisky but hates spiders; he has a naturally witty sense of humour and he enjoys chasing cats, particularly the cat who lives at Marlinspike and belongs to Captain Haddock.

Whether Hergé was trying to tell his ex-girlfriend something by naming a dog after her has never been established.

"Cheers!"

AND THEY CALL IT PUPPY LOVE

Best of breed: Dachshunds
The mutt of Manhattan

There's nothing like the pair of eyes on a Dachshund dog to melt the heart of even the coldest human being. They are so soulful and alluring; talk about a little boy lost. Aww, bless!

All this soppiness is all very well, but try telling badgers about Dachshunds being sweet and you'll find they'll strongly disagree. From their origin in Germany in the 1900s, Dachshunds have been used to chase and flush out badgers. And very good at this task they have proved to be. Well, they have a head start due

to their skinny build. Imagine a St Bernard trying to follow a badger down a hole. It would look ridiculous, wouldn't it?

Nowadays, the Dachshund is a popular companion dog, particularly in the USA.

Dachshunds. Well, not literally full but there are many of them walking its streets and avenues and adding to the charm of the place. Lively and playful, they are great fun and can live up to 17 years. Hurrah for the Dachshund!

Cartoon canines!
Pluto leads the way

The animation world has always enjoyed putting animals on the screen and has there ever been a more successful and enduring cartoon animal than the dog? Pluto first appeared in 1930 in an animation called *The Chain Gang*. He was clearly a wise networker – he became good mates with Mickey Mouse, who may have been just a mouse but was the most important character in the Walt Disney world!

Before long, Pluto's influence ensured that the cartoon world fell in love with dogs and Pluto was joined in animation kennel by Goofy, Deputy Dawg, Snoopy, Scooby-Doo, Scrappy-Doo, Muttley and many, many others. Given how much children adore dogs, the success of canine cartoon characters is not difficult to understand. Long may canines reign in the cartoon and comic world!

Once upon a time, a Rough Collie named Pal proved too energetic for his Californian owners and they sold him for five dollars. Before you weep for the little rascal, remember that every dog has his day. Pal was certainly about to have his: he became the most famous dog star of all time!

The character Lassie was created in 1938 by Collie-owning author Eric Knight for *Lassie Come Home*, a short story published in a UK newspaper. It went on to become a novel, a television series and a movie. Although Lassie is a female character, all nine Lassies have been played by male dogs because males have thicker coats and continue to look the part on screen even when they moult during the summer.

All nine were also direct descendants of Pal, who in his role as Lassie quickly became a global icon: he was the poster dog for the "Keep America Beautiful" campaign during the 1960s, visited the White House and was awarded a star on the Hollywood Walk of Fame. Ooh, get him! He was even given his own apartment. It really is a dog's life, isn't it?

Totally Toto!

Walkies down the yellow brick road!

All dog owners have on one occasion or another taken their pet out on a particularly eventful walk. But there have been few more eventful walks than that undertaken by Dorothy and her dog Toto in *The Wizard of Oz*. What with the cyclone, the witches, the scarecrow and the lion, it really was an exceptional stroll.

Toto was played by a Cairn Terrier called Terry and, even though the character was a boy in the show, Terry was actually a girl. Her owner, Carl Spitz, received a salary of $125 per week for Terry's work.

It has been suggested that there might be political undertones to the film, but how does Toto fit into all this? Well, dogs were often used in political cartoons to represent politicians or their parties. Could Toto be a representative of the teetotallers or Prohibitionists who were big on the political scene when the story was written? We haven't got a clue!

Just when you'd accepted that policemen and dogs work together to solve crimes, someone writes a story about policemen investigating crimes committed by dogs. What's all that about? At the beginning of the last century, perhaps the most famous Sherlock Holmes novel, *The Hound of the Baskervilles*, was published. It is the tale of an alleged curse that sees all members of the Baskerville family killed by a demonic dog.

Not that all were gobbled up; one was found dead in his garden with a terrified expression on his face. It would be natural to assume the poor chap simply collapsed with despair when the realization hit him of how horribly boring gardening is. But a trail of paw prints was seen near his body and it was thought that he died of a heart attack after being confronted by the huge hound. Anyway, Holmes and his assistant Dr Watson investigate and – quelle surprise – it all turns out to be a bit more complicated.

The story has been adapted for the screen 18 times. It's evocative stuff: try taking a walk across the Devon moors late one winter night and see if you don't literally soil yourself with fear.

Hitler's hound
Blondi voz only obeying orders

As we all know, dogs are obedient animals. They learn to respect their masters and follow their orders. There's none of that disobedience you get from other animals. Well, in wartime Germany there existed one German Shepherd called Blondi who quite literally "voz only obeying orders" – her master was Adolf Hitler.

Hitler was apparently very fond of Blondi and kept her by his side to the bitter end in his bunker during the fall of Berlin.

He even allowed her to sleep in his bedroom. "I love animals, especially dogs," he boasted. What a softie, eh?

However, one of the final acts of Hitler's life was to kill Blondi. As the Soviets closed in, Hitler decided he would commit suicide using cyanide pills before they could get to him. Worrying that the pills might not work, he tested one on Blondi.

Poor old Blondi. Not so much a man's best friend as a beast's best friend.

44 Opening the Iron Curtain

More courageous canines

The Second World War was a rough time for everyone – and all dogs, too. Within the first two months of food rationing beginning in Britain, over 200,000 dogs had died as families prioritized their stocks. Also, despite their heroic showings in the First World War, it was at first felt by some that dogs had no place in modern warfare.

How wrong they were. Before long, the government was appealing to households across the country to donate their dogs to the war effort. Dogs were used as sentries, messengers, mine-detectors and also "para-pups" who would jump from planes behind enemy lines to save stranded troops. One such dog, a black and white mongrel named Rob who wore a patch over one eye, made 20 such heroic jumps.

Also worthy of note is Chips, the German Shepherd Collie Husky mix who served with the US army and guarded numerous buildings, took hordes of enemies prisoner and sniffed out foes wherever they hid.

"Fancy having to go through all this again."

And what about Judy, an English Pointer who survived two years alongside her owner in a Japanese POW camp? The Japanese tried to shoot her several times, but she toughed it out and was eventually released.

Moving stuff, isn't it? Go on, put the book down and have a good old weep.

You know, older doesn't automatically equal wiser. The Afghan Hound is one of the oldest dog breeds about, dating back to pre-Christian times at least. However, this breed is also thought to be one of the least intelligent of dogs. Sorry, guys.

Another characteristic of the Afghan Hound is that they possess a strong independent streak. Some have even compared the dog in this regard to cats – and insults don't come much harsher than that in the canine world.

So let's try and be a bit nice, yes? Well, the Afghan Hound is a relatively healthy dog that can live for 14 years or more. And anyone who has seen an Afghan Hound in full flight knows that it is a truly awesome sight.

Perhaps the most impressive fact about this breed, though, is that unlike humans they managed to exist in Afghanistan without making a complete mess of it. Many human beings from America, Russia and indeed some Afghans can't say that. Maybe they should just all give up their fighting and let the Hounds take over! Dog power!

46 Dennis's dog
The life and times of Gnasher!

Paper boys across the country regularly risk getting their fingers bitten off by territorial dogs as they put various publications through people's doors – and since 1938, many paper boys have been delivering the *Beano*.

Some 30 years into the *Beano's* life, its star character Dennis the Menace was joined by his faithful dog Gnasher, an Abyssinian Wire-Haired Tripe Hound. At first, Gnasher was a rather terrifying little mutt, but as the years have progressed he has become increasingly cute and cuddly.

More recently, Gnasher has fathered a son called Gnipper who appears alongside his dad in a new strip. Between them, they are in and out of mischief all the time. Gnasher has also fathered daughters called Gnancy, Gnatasha, Gnaomi, Gnanette and Gnora – see what they did there?! – but the five girls rarely show up in the *Beano* as they live with their mum.

The breakdown of the modern family is frightfully upsetting and when the shocking decline of family values has even hit the Gnasher clan, it's fair to say that we should all take a long, hard look at ourselves.

A Waggly Tale
How Much Is That Doggie In The Window?

They say a cynic knows the price of everything and the value of nothing. Well the American composer and lyricist Bob Merrill can't have been cynical because he didn't even know the price of that doggie in the window. You know, the one with the waggly tail.

Just in case you are wondering what the hell we're talking about, Merrill was the man who, in 1952, wrote the popular song "How Much is that Doggie in the Window?" The song has gone on to become a worldwide classic with the most popular versions recorded by Patti Page and Lita Roza.

The song concerns a woman who has to take a trip to California and wants to buy a dog so her boyfriend won't be lonely while she is away. It might just be our depraved imaginations but we can't help worrying that she had something deeply unsavoury in mind. Leave the dogs out of it for goodness sake!

Queen's Pembroke Corgis
Royal family values

What is the best birthday present you ever got? Well, when the Queen turned 18 she got what is probably her favourite birthday present ever – a Corgi! When she was presented with Susan back in 1944, little did anyone know that this was the start of a love affair that would endure longer than any of the toe-sucking, bulimia-dominated, let's-all-cheat-on-each-other relationships that most of her relatives have had.

The Queen has owned 30 Corgis down the years and many of them have been direct descendants of Susan. As she travels between Buckingham Palace, Windsor Castle, Sandringham and Balmoral – tough life, huh? – she takes her beloved pets with her.

Despite the Queen's loyalty to her Corgis, there has been some lust in the air and when some of them got jiggy with Princess Anne's Dachshunds, they produced a cross-breed that has become known as the "Dorgi" – "Dorgi" is also probably how the Queen pronounces the word "doggy".

Friends of the Queen tell proudly of how, despite her power and regal blood, the Queen insists on feeding her dogs herself. Wow, she really is one of the people, isn't she?

True class

Lady and the Tramp hits the big screen

It was Tony Blair who said "We're all middle-class now." Whether the spectacular-toothed politician was correct or not, he couldn't have said that in the 1950s when *Lady and the Tramp* hit the big screen. The 15th animated film to emerge from the Disney stable, it was the tale of an unlikely romance between a posh dog and a down-at-heel mutt who lives on the streets.

Lady is a lovely and pampered Cocker Spaniel, whereas Tramp is a mixed-breed stray. The pair meet and share adventures together and eventually fall in love, causing everyone watching to sob tears of sheer joy.

Feeling a bit emotional just writing this, actually. Why can't we knock down all these barriers that divide us and all just get on? We're all flesh and blood underneath it all and have much more in common than we may think. Come on, let's just all get together and love each other and forget our differences. (Have you been drinking again? – Ed.)

An intergalactic walkies
The first dog in space

Once upon a time, a stray mongrel female was minding her own business on the streets of Moscow when she was approached by a government official who asked her: "Fancy popping up into space?"

And so it was in 1957 that Laika became the first dog to take a walkies into the cosmos.

Of course, Laika wasn't really asked if she fancied the space trip and therein lies the controversy

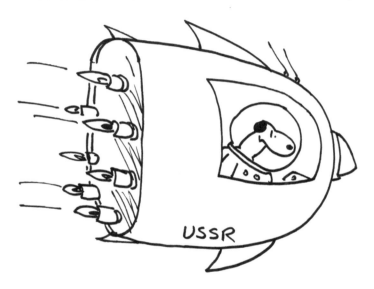

USSR

at the heart of this story. Although it was hoped that sending her up in the spacecraft Sputnik 2 would reveal all sorts of facts about the prospects for human space travel, many felt that it was cruel to send a dog to certain death in this way. The Canine Defence League called for all dog lovers to observe a minute's silence for Laika.

Although the Soviet authorities said that Laika died painlessly a week into the mission, it later turned out that those nasty Commies were lying (remember this was pre-1989, when all Russians were still bad). In reality, Laika died a few hours after take-off from panic and overheating.

A minute's silence for Laika, please.

Hobo's in the house!

Television's most touching dog?

Forget about reading *How to Win Friends and Influence People* by Dale Carnegie if you want to learn how to make everyone adore you, just watch an episode of *The Littlest Hobo*! *The Littlest Hobo* was originally a movie made in 1958 and was then turned into a black-and-white television series in the 1960s. A new version of the series began in 1979.

In each episode, the title character – a dog, as you've probably guessed – would arrive somewhere and find people who were down on their luck and solve all their problems before moving on to the next town. He knew how to make himself loved! He once parachuted from an aeroplane with medicine to save a boy's life – but we've all done that at some point in our lives, haven't we? Six different German Shepherds played the part of the Hobo and among the human actors in the series was Mike Myers, who went on to find fame in the Austin Powers series.

Most memorable about the show is probably the theme tune. So, all together now: "Maybe tomorrow, I'll want to settle down. Until tomorrow, I'll just keep moving on." Love it!

THE Daily Dog

THE FILTH AND THE FURY!

THE MORAL MAJORITY SLAM SOOTY!

Exclusive by our ROVER REPORTER

Middle England was in outrage last night over the children's television show *Sooty*. The programme-makers were accused of corrupting impressionable children with pro-sex propaganda. They were also slammed for promoting anti-police messages!

A man from Tunbridge Wells – who asked to remain anonymous – told us: "By introducing Sooty's girlfriend, Soo, the programme sends out a message that sex is OK. The way we're going, every kid in Britain will be gay or pregnant – or both! – before the year is out!"

He added: "When Sooty hits PC Nab over the head with a hammer, the clear message being given to our children is 'Why not go and kill police officers?'"

Also inside: Richard Littlebrain asks: Is Sooty more evil than asylum seekers?

53 The Belle of the ball!
TV's French revolution

During the 1960s, most people wandered around smashed off their faces on drugs 24 hours a day. A slight exaggeration, perhaps, but exaggerations can be fun. However, for those who didn't indulge, there was the joy of *Belle and Sebastian* on BBC2. The show was based on the series of French novels called *Belle et Sebastien*, which told of the mountain-based adventures of Sebastien and his huge white dog. Eventually, an animated version was also produced, which became a huge hit across the world.

The influence of the series has even reached the world of rock, where Scottish indie band Belle & Sebastian are named after the initial series. Proof yet again that dogs rock!

BARKING UP THE WRONG TREE

Best of breed: Foxhounds

Recipe for a hunting dog

Simply take a nice fast Greyhound, a Fox Terrier with its hunting instinct and a tenacious little Bulldog. Scrunch 'em all together and the result is the English Foxhound. That's just the recipe that was whipped up during the reign of Henry VIII in the 1500s. They were used for deer and fox hunting and they proved excellent in that field.

It was once the case that English Foxhounds from different regions across England had different strengths. Those from Yorkshire were fastest, those in Staffordshire had deeper voices. This was a sort of canine precursor to the rivalries played out in football today.

The English Foxhound gets along with humans and with other animals, including horses. Another very active dog, the Foxhound also has an incredible sense of smell – a useful characteristic on the hunt, of course. Full of energy, it enjoys running and will, in fact, run and run – much like most of the jokes in this book.

This breed is also a fantastic guard dog, although it must be said they are rarely kept as domestic pets. Following recent legislation banning hunting with dogs, foxhounds are at a bit of a loose end. So if you ever see one, don't be surprised if rather than saying "Woof" it says "Gissajob"!

Alas Smith and bones!

Dodie does delightful dog books

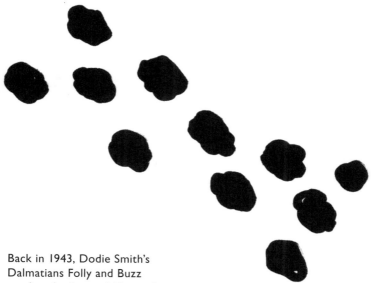

Back in 1943, Dodie Smith's Dalmatians Folly and Buzz produced a litter of 15 puppies, one of which was on the brink of death during the birth but was brought back to life by her husband Alec. This rather icky image provided the inspiration for a scene in her novel *The Hundred and One Dalmatians*, which came out 13 years later and was instantly declared a classic. The novel was adapted for the big screen first in 1961 and again in 1996.

She also wrote another, less-known, novel about dogs called *Starlight Barking*, which loosely represents a sequel to *Dalmatians*, in which a dog from the original book has become a friend of the prime minister.

It was a good job that Smith concentrated on writing about dogs, because when she spoke about other animals, the results could be perplexing. "The family, that dear octopus from whose tentacles we never quite escape, nor in our innermost hearts never quite wish to," she once mused. Yeah, right: whatever, Dodie!

You ain't nothin' but a hound dog

Canine Elvis impersonator seen in Sainsbury's

As anyone who has found themselves stranded at home on a rainy afternoon will know, the worldwide web is a cauldron of bizarre and frankly sinister things. We've all received those emails offering us all manner of saucy and strange things and we've all stumbled upon some pretty freaky websites. Don't pretend you haven't.

However, perhaps the weirdest thing on sale in cyber land is the Elvis Presley dog costume. Yes, you read that correctly. For little more than the cost of a decent bottle of wine, you can dress your dog up as the King in this shiny satin suit, complete with fake hands. Of course, whether you would actually want to do this is entirely a matter for you and your conscience.

Presley himself was an animal lover who owned chickens, a monkey, horses and dogs. Among his dogs was a Chow called Getlo and a Collie called Baba. Dogs must have always been on his mind because he even recorded a song about them. His hit single "Hound Dog", released in 1956, sold four million copies. Later, he released the lesser-known song "Dog's Life". Let's rock!

Magic moments
Dougal and the roundabout

The French have given us many things down the years: frogs' legs, men cycling around in stripy jumpers with strings of onions around their necks, David Ginola and – of course – *'Allo! 'Allo!* However, the greatest cultural donation to hop across the channel was *The Magic Roundabout*. Originally a French show entitled *Le Manège Enchanté*, *The Magic Roundabout* enlivened many a British tea-time during the 1960s and '70s.

Starring alongside Zebedee, Brian, Ermintrude, Dylan and Florence was Dougal, a shaggy-haired dog. Dougal was a rather grumpy little animal, and it is thought by some that his character was based in part on Tony Hancock. Others think he was based on French politician Charles de Gaulle. Some even think the whole show was based on some sort of psychedelic drug trip. Surely not!

Whatever or whoever Dougal was based on, his world-weary humour was a hit with adults and children alike. Felicitations to the French!

Lost and hound!

Pickles recovers stolen trophy

Forget the three lions, what about the, erm, one dog? In 1966, four months before the first football World Cup held in England kicked off, the famous Jules Rimet trophy was stolen from an exhibition in Central Hall, Westminster. As a sentence containing the words "piss-up" and "brewery" echoed around the rest of the footballing globe, a dog called Pickles proved the old maxim: "Cometh the hour, cometh the dog".

While being taken on a walk one Sunday evening in south-east London – and how many other tales of heroism have taken place on a Sunday evening in that part of the world? None, that's how many! – Pickles sniffed out the trophy under a bush, where it lay wrapped in newspaper. His owner David Corbett took it to Cannon Row police station and the scene was set for England's triumphant World Cup performance that summer.

More recently, Olympic rower James Cracknell had his stolen gold medals returned to him by a dog. Gosh, these mutts really are good at getting our sporting heroes out of a pickle, aren't they? Indeed, one can't help wondering whether just as dogs solve these crimes, it might be cat burglars that commit them! (Do stop rabbiting on – Ed.)

The Fab Paws!

Never mind the Beatles, here are the Beagles!

The Beatles preferred to sing about blackbirds, piggies, octopi and racoons instead of dogs, but a number of Beatles tribute bands have hilariously and imaginatively named themselves the Beagles. Meanwhile, Beatles memorabilia shops offer cuddly toy dogs dressed in Beatles garb.

We'd obviously prefer not to descend into cheap doggy puns based on titles of well-known Beatles songs, but one can't help wonder what tracks might be on the set-list of a band called the Beagles. Oh go on, just a few then: "When I'm Sixty-Paw", "A Dog in the Life", "The Ballad of John and Fido", "I am the Woof Woof", "You've Got to Hide Your Bone Away" and "I Wanna Hold Your Hound". (Stop it at once – Ed.)

Palatable Pavlov

Digest this, readers!

There are certain dinner party conversations that you can guarantee will always come up when you gather a load of poncey, self-satisfied people round a table with nice food and fine wine. House prices is one, what everyone does for a living is another. Well, if you'd ever had Ivan Petrovich Pavlov round for dinner – he'd probably have started discussing the digestive systems of dogs! Yuck!

Now, we grant you that it is unlikely that you're going to have Pavlov round to eat – he died in 1936 – but our point remains valid. He won a Nobel Prize for his research into the digestive system of dogs. In short, he discovered that when dogs are presented with food, they salivate before the food actually reaches their mouths.

This might not seem an earth-shattering discovery in these modern and decadent times. But back then, it was truly exciting stuff. It created the concept of "conditioning" which unlocked all sorts of stuff to do with our understanding of psychology. "Pavlovian thinking" was also a big influence on Aldous Huxley's novel *Brave New World*.

In the 1970s, a prog-rock band called Pavlov's Dog was formed in St Louis. They didn't do all that well. Funny that – you would have thought with such a catchy name they would have conquered the world. No, seriously, what a great name! You are truly rock 'n' roll, guys!

Best of breed: Poodles

Tricky Dicky's mutt of choice

Poodles may look like sweet little creatures, but beneath that cute exterior lies a dark and sinister truth. OK, that's exaggerating slightly, but Poodles are not the pretty little pushovers they may seem on the surface. For instance, Poodles are fantastic bird hunters and if you asked representatives of the bird community what they thought of Poodles, they certainly wouldn't say "Ah, they're such sweet little things!" Neither would drug pushers, who have been busted many a time by Poodles used by French customs.

Enough of the militant Poodle-detractors, what about their history?

Most believe that the Poodle's origins lie in France in the 1500s, but others argue it may have come from Russia or Germany. They have been popularly used as entertainment in circuses and as fashion accessories.

Known as one of the more intelligent breeds, Poodles are fantastic companions even though they do retain a somewhat independent personality.

Everyone from Miss Piggy of *The Muppet Show* and former US President Richard Nixon has owned one. And if that doesn't prove how great they are, what does?

Sheepdog Saturday

One man and his dog

Down the years, there have been many ways to pass a few weekend hours in front of the box. Sniggering at Dickie Davis when he presented *World of Sport*, praying that there will be some huge crash on *Ski Sunday*, sneering at the ridiculously easy questions on *Bullseye* and – of course – slashing your wrists in front of the *EastEnders* omnibus.

Happy days, indeed. However, for many the highlight of the weekend television schedule was *One Man and His Dog*. No, this wasn't some sinister porn flick. It was on the BBC rather than Five, after all. In fact it was a sheepdog trial show that started in the 1970s and pulled in over eight million viewers at its peak.

The name of the show was later used by the makers of yet another of those cockney crime films that have attempted to cash in on the success of the *Lock, Stock* series. But who needs crime when you can watch dogs guiding sheep around?

"Oh, do stop being such a bunch of idiots!" This is quite literally what dogs would probably say to humans if they had the chance to comment on our reaction to the rabies virus. Still today, across Britain, people worry about catching rabies from dogs. This is despite the fact that 99 per cent of human rabies deaths occur in Africa, Asia and South America.

It's also despite the fact that rabies is not just transmitted from dogs; bats, bears, cats, ferrets and organ transplants have also left human beings suffering from rabies. And do we see human beings fleeing across parks in sheer terror at the thought of organ transplants? No, that would be silly, wouldn't it?

Still, we all love a good panic and many in Britain were foaming at the mouth with excitement during the 1970s when fears over rabies increased. This panic was the forerunner of the terror over dangerous dogs that occurred during the 1990s. (The 1980s were strangely free of dog-related hysteria. Maybe we were all too busy trying to work out how to blame AIDS on dogs.)

The Blue Border Collie!

Shep shows up

The year 1971 was great for Border Collies. For it was that year in which Shep joined the *Blue Peter* team. An excitable little rascal, Shep would often jump up at his owner, John Noakes, and in doing so prompted a new catchphrase. There's really only one more thing to say. So, all together now: "Get down, Shep!"

65 Rolling in it
The Andrex puppies

When a dog's gotta go, a dog's gotta go and most dog-owners will recall a time when their beloved pet squatted down and answered the call of nature in embarrassing circumstances. Dogs don't always get the etiquette of lavatory-use, do they?

It is, therefore, rather fitting that when Labradors were chosen to advertise Andrex toilet tissue, they still managed to make a mess in most of the commercials. However, the Andrex puppies are truly adorable and it is impossible not to forgive the little darlings for leaving trails of toilet paper everywhere. After all, it could be worse. It could be used toilet paper they leave around the house. Ewww.

66 Massive mutt

The big dog on the big screen

Be careful what you feed your dog. When an Old English Sheepdog ate a bowl of Project X – an experimental growth formula – it became quite literally the biggest dog in the world. Chaos and hilarity ensued as everyone tried to collar him!

We should explain that this isn't a real story, just a tale that was made up for cinema called *Digby: the Biggest Dog in the World*. All the same, this was the canine world's answer to *King Kong* and

was a great film, an absolute howl, in fact. It could almost be said that you would be absolutely barking to miss it. And if you ask us, an overgrown dog is far preferable to an overgrown ape so this film absolutely lifts its leg all over *King Kong*. OK?

Cartoon colour controversy!

What colour was Roobarb? Who cares?

There are some topics that always guarantee heated debate: hunting, religion, capital punishment and the Middle East are just some of these. However, the most fierce debate in the history of humankind is what colour Roobarb the cartoon dog is. Roobarb was the star of the BBC cartoon of the same name that ran before the early-evening news in the 1970s. Starring alongside Custard the cat, he was always in some scrape or another. Drawn in rough style, the pair were great entertainment throughout the 30 episodes of the series and we really should have just been content to have been treated to such a great show.

However, since the pair left our screens, debate has raged about what colour Roobarb was. Some say he was green, some say he was yellow. It is terrifying to think that grown adults could actually get so excited about this issue. Some people really need to get out more.

68 Beagle mania

Pups made to puff

Would you like a cigarette? No thanks, I don't smoke. We humans take for granted our right to not smoke if we don't want to. What a shame that we've denied so many dogs that same right.

During the 1950s, people started speculating that there was a link between smoking and lung cancer. At this point, any sensible human being would, if they smoked, have immediately stopped smoking. However, some silly people carried on smoking. And some nasty human beings decided to experiment on Beagles to see if they could find out more about the subject.

And so it was that hundreds of Beagles were routinely trapped inside small boxes and force-fed cigarette after cigarette. Although the end result was that these tests proved the link between smoking and cancer, which then led to British cigarette manufacturers putting warnings on their packets, many feel that the cruelty inflicted on these Beagles was unjustifiable.

A piano pedigree!
Rowlf stars in *The Muppets*

It's easy to lose count of how many animals have risen from an appearance on a dog food commercial to international stardom – let's see, there must be at least … one of them! Rowlf the dog first appeared on a television advert for Purina Dog Chow in 1962. Then he popped up with a cameo performance on *Sesame Street* before his big break on *The Muppet Show*.

A scruffy little brown mutt with long floppy ears, Rowlf was the resident pianist and a big fan of Ludwig van Beethoven. He would sometimes wear a tuxedo when he sat tickling the ivories.

It is believed that Rowlf was Jim Henson's favourite character. We'd bloody hope so! With his sense of humour and musical genius, Rowlf was the real star of the show and left Kermit and Miss Piggy completely in the shade!

Rowlf went on a walkies down the hall of fame as the Muppets hit Hollywood with films like *The Muppets Take Manhattan*. In recent years, sightings of the little mutt have been few and far between. So next time you are lounging around in a hotel bar and you hear someone playing the piano, have a quick check. It could be Rowlf!

Counselling canines!

The therapy dog

Human beings are rubbish therapists. All we seem capable of is listening with a patronizing expression on our faces before concluding that it is all linked to the time we sat on the potty as a child. And we charge for this "service"!

Dogs, however, are excellent therapists and have been officially recognized as such since 1976 when American nurse Elaine Smith noticed while working in England how the health of patients improved after a visit from a Golden Retriever. On her return to America, she created a training programme for dogs and the era of the therapy dog began!

Hospitals across the world are regularly visited by dogs that bring joy to patients by performing tricks or simply just by being hugged and lovable. There are also therapy cats, rabbits and birds. But none is as good as therapy dogs because, as we keep establishing in these pages, dogs are better than all other types of animals put together. I mean, would you want to tell a rabbit or a bird about any problems you are having in your sex life?

Best of breed: St Bernards

Is the barrel just a crock?

The image of a St Bernard bounding up to a poor soul stranded in the snow of the Alps and offering it a swig of brandy from the barrel around its neck is an enduring one. It's also quite possibly a load of old balderdash, unfortunately. Descendants of the monks whom we mentioned earlier in connection with the origin of the rescue dog insist that St Bernards never wore barrels around their necks, and there is debate as to whether any of them actually rescued any stranded travellers.

However, what is certain is that St Bernards are huge and muscular dogs, which is why they have been used a lot for hauling. They can be over 70cm tall and can weigh up to 90kg and as such can be effective guard dogs. This is, however, more because of their intimidating bulk than their nature, which is normally gentle.

Living for up to 11 years, St Bernards are great dogs if you don't mind a huge hulk of a dog plodding around your home. And if you want to put a barrel of brandy around its neck – doing that would certainly liven up a walk in the park – then no one, not even monks, can stop you.

Doctor, Dogtor

Who is K-9?

Where did K-9 come from? Making his debut in 1977, the first K-9 was created by Professor Marius, who worked for the Bi-Al Foundation on an asteroid near Titan in the year 5000. Don't worry, we haven't gone mad; K-9 was a fictional robot dog who starred in *Doctor Who*!

In case you haven't guessed, the name K-9 is a play on the word "canine", but if you think that's a weak gag, get this – it was originally going to be called FIDO, an acronym (almost) of Phenomenal Indication Data Observation. Blimey.

K-9 was a loyal friend to Tom Baker's Doctor Who between 1977 and 1981 and rejoined the cast in 2006. Luckily, K-9 was Tardis-trained and so he never used the police box as a toilet. Unlike a nation of boozers who have a slash in phone-boxes most nights as they get caught short on their way back from the pub.

Can you Spot him?
Literature's most elusive puppy

Dog detectives are appealing for information that will lead to the discovery of the whereabouts of Spot the dog. First published in 1980, *Where's Spot* is a series of children's books where the reader searches for Spot by lifting various flaps on the pages. It has since become a cartoon and a worldwide success, translated into more than 60 languages.

Spot the dog is described as a yellow puppy with brown spots on his body and a brown tip on his tail. Any help in finding Spot would be much appreciated.

Bossy Barbara
The Woodhouse way

For the first 70 years of her life, Barbara Woodhouse lived a pretty routine existence. Then, in 1980, she appeared on television and became a household name. Her show was called *Training Dogs the Woodhouse Way* and featured the no-nonsense Woodhouse bossing everyone around while wearing a woollen kilt.

It is fitting that Barbara Woodhouse was a star during the 1980s because her bossy manner was reminiscent of Maggie Thatcher, who was British prime minister in that decade. And, just like Thatcher, Woodhouse was the subject of much controversy. Many believed her techniques were too

strict and forceful but, in her defence, she trained over 17,000 dogs and managed to make many naughty or unhappy dogs behave much better.

Cesar Milan, who runs a dog psychology centre in Los Angeles has provoked similar controversy.

However, the final word goes to Woodhouse. She managed to put a nasty image in everyone's minds when she said: "I've caught more ills from people sneezing over me and giving me viral infections than from kissing dogs."

Ewww, enough already.

Who dunnit?

The Dingo dunnit!

In 1980, Australian baby Azaria Chamberlain went missing during a camping trip with her family. The original inquest into her death found she had been killed by a Dingo. Then, it was decided that her mother Lindy might have cut Azaria's throat and she was sent to trial and convicted of murder. Then after new evidence emerged, Lindy was cleared and released. The case remains unsolved, but most people now believe that a Dingo was responsible for Azaria's death.

This case was the trial of the century in Australia and attracted huge attention. It has now entered popular culture, with both a feature film and a movie joining a host of books about the case. There have also been jokes galore about it on television programmes from *Frasier* to *Seinfeld*. When Aussie rock musician Ben Folds ditched his band and went solo, he called his first tour "A Dingo Took My Band".

It's great that people feel there is so much humour to be had in this topic. After all, it was only a nine-week-old girl who bled to death, and if you can't laugh about that, what can you laugh at?

76 The glamour gal!
Brigitte backs dogs

She might have been known as a "sex kitten" at the height of her fame but Brigitte Bardot loves all animals, including dogs. Among her many campaigns on behalf of canines, she has lobbied Russian president Vladimir Putin asking him to ban dog-fighting and she successfully saved over 100,000 Romanian stray dogs from death.

Some accuse Bardot – who in 1986 established the Brigitte Bardot Foundation for the Welfare and Protection of Animals – of being a misanthrope who actually prefers the company of animals to that of humans. And what's wrong with that?

As we learned earlier, Bardot was born in the Chinese Year of the Dog, but she has some words of advice for China and other countries where dogs are eaten: "Cows are grown to be eaten, dogs are not."

No more canine cards
The dog licence is abolished

DOG CERTIFICATE

This is to certify that ———————
is a registered dog owned by ———————

Breed: ———————— Sex: ————

Age: ——— Colour & markings: ————

Name of vet: ————————

Signed: ————————

This is to certify that dog licences existed in the UK until 1987, but up until the licence's abolition over half of dog owners were rumoured to be flouting the regulation anyway. This, despite the fact that licences cost only 37p when they were abolished. How tight are some people? Nowadays a lot of dog owners choose to have their pets chipped.

78 Neighbourly love

Bouncer bosses the soap world

There have been some gripping storylines in soap operas down the years: Who shot JR?; Michelle Fowler's pregnancy; the Brookside siege; and what will Hilda cook Stan for his tea tonight? However, for dog lovers, one of soap's most dramatic moments came in *Neighbours* when Bouncer was asked to choose between Mrs Mangel and Mike Young. The pair had been squabbling over who should care for Bouncer and the Labrador chose Mrs Mangel over Mike (played by Guy Pearce, he of the high cheekbones).

Bouncer was a truly heroic dog. He saved the life of Madge Bishop (played by Anne Charleston, she of the croaky voice) when he barked down the phone and alerted the authorities to a fire at the Mangel household. He was nominated for a bravery reward for this moment of courage.

British soap dogs are rubbish in comparison. There was Roly who belonged to Dirty Den in *EastEnders* (played by Leslie Grantham, he of the lewd webcam photos) and Wellard, who was owned by Robbie Jackson (played by Dean Gaffney, he of the rather canine facial features). But neither of these had the, erm, bounce of Bouncer!

"I was in *EastEnders* but I didn't want to get typecast."

Best of breed: Jack Russells

Family favourite

The Jack Russell Terrier is one of the most visible and recognized of dogs. Energetic and snappy little creatures, their occasional outbursts of aggression should not detract from their loving and affectionate personalities.

Originating in Great Britain in the 1800s, Jack Russells were originally used to locate foxes and badgers that had gone underground. Nowadays, they are popular pets that can regularly be seen straining at the leash as their owners approach a park or field.

Living for up to 15 years, Jack Russells have few health problems and are great pets for families that have the time and energy to give them plenty

of exercise and play. If under-exercised, these dogs can quickly develop a number of behavioural problems.

This is also a very famous breed that has appeared on film and in television – perhaps the most notable being Eddie, the dog belonging to Martin Crane in the hit sitcom *Frasier*. It's little wonder that this breed is so popular on the screen; it positively oozes personality. However, one of the most famous Jack Russells wasn't even a dog. It was a human being. Step forward and take a wicket, Robert Charles Russell, known as Jack Russell to cricket fans everywhere. Owzat?!

He feels like a woman!
Spuds MacKenzie

Lager, huh? Isn't it just the most manly of drinks? Life doesn't get any more manly than sitting down and necking a nice chilled lager, does it? Quite fitting then that Budweiser chose a really laddish Bull Terrier to advertise their product! Spuds MacKenzie was always surrounded by lovely females and was a true jack the lad. The ultimate party animal, he hung out with babes in a hot tub, went water-skiing and performed elaborate drum solos.

What a man, what a man, what a mighty fine man! The only problem was that Spuds was actually a girl! Just as with other famous dogs – including Lassie, although admittedly the other way round – the producers picked a female dog to play a male part. When Honey Tree Evil Eye (the improbable real name of Spuds) had to answer the call of nature, the producers had to hide her from the cameras, lest her lady's parts be recognized.

Honey died of kidney failure in 1993 at the age of 10. We all raise a glass of foaming lager to him. Sorry, her.

Hooch loves ya?

Turner turns dog-lover

The witness protection scheme has a major flaw in it – it applies only to humans! So when Hooch, a large French Mastiff, witnesses a brutal murder, the police in the movie *Turner & Hooch* have to take him in to protect him from being "put down" before the killer can be caught.

Naturally, this 1989 comedy film, starring Tom Hanks as detective Scott Turner, soon descends into high farce as Hooch tests Turner's patience by wrecking his home and generally turning his life upside down.

One of the better comedy films involving a dog, this is well worth a look and features one of the greatest on-screen performances from a dog ever seen. Tom Hanks isn't that bad, either!

In the dog house!

Blunkett's guide dog enters parliament

When the world learned about former Home Secretary David Blunkett's colourful love life, nobody was surprised. After all, Blunkett oozes the kind of sex appeal that unites all genders and sexualities in sheer pant-wetting arousal. Not since the days of the equally gorgeous David Mellor has an MP turned so many on. It's safe to say we'd all like a bit of Blunkett action.

However, nobody got as close to the Labour lothario as his faithful guide dogs. The first of these was Teddy, who became the first dog to enter the House of Commons chamber. Another one – Lucy, a black curly coat Retriever – once vomited in the chamber during a speech by Blunkett's Conservative opposite number. No manners, but what a critic! Her half-sister Sadie replaced Lucy in 2003.

Anyway, all this talk about the pin-up that is David Blunkett has got us quite beside ourselves with excitement. So let's move on to the next topic!

83 The dog ate it!

Blaming everything on the mutt

Dogs have so many wonderful uses and one of the best of all is that you can blame them for all manner of things. No, we're not referring to people who when they pass wind blame the resultant stench on their dog (and incidentally, nobody associated with this book would ever dream of doing such a thing). Instead, we're talking about that great line: "The dog ate it."

The traditional use of this line is by a naughty schoolboy on a Monday morning when he is asked by his teacher where his homework is. However, there is no reason why you have to stop using it when you leave school. Residents in Stroud, Gloucestershire, have adapted it to get out of paying rent by simply telling their council: "The dog ate our rent card." Genius.

There was once a hilariously witty punch-line to this page. But we can't bring it to you – the dog ate it.

Listen, this is serious! We are literally ALL going to die! We have only moments left on this planet – so make the most of them by reading this page! No, a nuclear bomb is not about to drop on your head, nor is a gargantuan meteor about to strike Earth. The truth is even more awful than that: someone has spotted a dog being taken for a walk. Oh dear, we are all doomed.

The above paragraph may appear to be the result of some ghastly cocktail of recreational drugs, but it is actually a fair reflection of the climate of fear in Britain in the early 1990s when dogs became the most dangerous and evil creatures ever to walk God's Earth. At least they were if you believed the newspapers, whose front pages regularly featured photographs of kids whose faces had been chomped by Rottweilers or Pit Bulls.

Panic broke out across the country as a result of these sensationalist reports – we needed someone to take a lead and calm us all down. Over to you, politicians …

85 The Commons touch

MPs pass panic act!

Whenever the press panics about anything, we can always depend on our MPs to maintain a level head. Yeah, right! As the aforementioned headlines about dangerous dogs caused public alarm, our MPs responded with the Dangerous Dogs Act of 1991. Whether this legislation represented a sensible step or an over-the-top response to an exaggerated threat is a matter of debate.

It became illegal to own Pit Bull Terriers, Tosas, Dogo Argentinos or Fila Brasileiros without a specific exemption from a court. Even then, the dog would have to be muzzled and kept on a lead at all times. No sort of life, really.

For many, the legislation was passed too hastily and "Dangerous Dogs Act" has become a by-word in parliamentary circles for any piece of legislation that has been rushed through without sensible consideration.

Still, in the twenty-first century, "dangerous" dogs have long been overtaken in the race to become the most vilified of living creatures by asylum seekers, reality television contestants and George W. Bush.

Pet passports!
Quarantine lifted for dogs

In February 2000, a new era in dog travel arrived when pet passports were introduced. For the first time in more than 100 years, dogs could enter the United Kingdom without having to go into quarantine for six months. Hurrah! The dogs could finally come on holiday abroad with us!

With cases of rabies in humans virtually unheard of in Britain – there had only been one in 25 years and that was the result of a woman being bitten by a bat – the government introduced the pet passports scheme, which meant dogs and cats could skip quarantine, provided they passed certain tests and were chipped.

However, as anyone who has queued at passport control after a long flight will know, sometimes just passing through an airport can feel like the equivalent of six months in quarantine.

Best of breed: Spaniels
Flush with success

If you want to catch a bird, then get yourself a Spaniel. Fear not, dear reader, we have not resorted to some sort of ghastly lads'-mag lingo about impressing ladies; we mean that if you want to catch an actual bird – you know, the feathered type – then a Spaniel would be a great help.

Be it Springer Spaniels, Cocker Spaniels or Cavalier King Charles Spaniels, these dogs are great fun. Most Spaniels have drop ears and eyes to die for that make them simply irresistible to dog-lovers and indeed anyone with a pulse.

Developed by British breeders, most Spaniels are gun dogs which were created to flush out birds from the undergrowth. (That's why we said that stuff about

birds.) But nowadays they are popular pets. Generally eager to please and great with children, they lap up love like few other creatures on this planet.

With a propensity to become spoilt thanks to their cute floppy ears and adorable, pleading eyes, the Spaniels are a great bunch of dogs. On that point everyone – apart from our feathered friends – would agree.

A right royal mess!

Princess Anne's terrifying Terriers

In 2002, a new wave of patriotism and pro-monarchy feeling swept the UK as we celebrated the Queen's Golden Jubilee. As we roamed the streets, giddily waving Union flags, what could possibly happen to spoil this renewed sense of love we felt for our royals?

Enter Dotty, an English Bull Terrier. In 2002, while Princess Anne was walking Dotty in Windsor Great Park, he attacked two children, one of whom was left with a bite on his collarbone and two on his left leg. The princess was convicted under the Dangerous Dogs Act, fined

£500 and ordered to pay £500 in damages to the children.

So, that's that dealt with then. Not so fast. The following year, one of the Queen's Corgis had to be put down after one of Princess Anne's Bull Terriers savaged it at Sandringham at Christmastime. The Queen was not amused.

For our part, we mourn the passing of the Queen's Corgi, but praise all of the royal dogs for being able – on the whole – to exist alongside the rather equine people who make up the royal family. Rarely have horse and hound co-existed so well!

The White House woofers!
Bush's awe of Terriers

It was Bill Clinton who said: "If you want a friend in Washington, you have to get a dog." Clinton duly acquired a chocolate Labrador Retriever called Buddy and he was right about the importance of woofers in Washington: the White House has seen many presidents down the years and nearly as many dogs!

Theodore Roosevelt owned three dogs: a Chesapeake Bay Retriever, a mongrel and also a Bull Terrier that was banned from the White House because it bit so many people. Lyndon Johnson had two Beagles called Him and Her. Ronald Reagan had a Cavalier King Charles Spaniel called Rex who lived in a lavish doghouse with photos of Ronnie and Nancy on the walls.

George W. Bush's Scottish Terrier Barney is a playful little boy who enjoys playing with soccer balls and golf balls. The White House website features four films starring Barney. Perhaps Barney Searches for the Weapons of Mass Destruction could be the next one?

Walkies on the wild side!

The Osbournes' dogs

Dogs might be a man's best friend, but ladies are pretty keen on the little rascals, too – and none more so than the queen of rock herself, Sharon Osbourne. Alongside Ozzy, Jack and Kelly, Sharon's seven dogs starred in the hit MTV show *The Osbournes*. An episode of the show was not complete without at least one member of the family having to step over a dropping or wade through a puddle of dog wee. Watching the dogs send Ozzy into ever deeper paroxysms of rage was great fun – particularly the time when the Osbourne mansion was invaded by fleas.

More recently, Sharon has been a judge on the reality pop show *The X Factor*, and in between throwing glasses of water over fellow judge Louis Walsh, perving over contestant Shane Ward and having a pop at Rebecca Loos, she has been known to bring her favourite dog Minnie into the studio. "Minnie is the top diva in my house," gushes Sharon. Wow, to be named the top diva in that house really is an accolade. When asked what he thinks of Minnie, Ozzy lifted the dog's backside to his nose, sniffed and commented: "There's the smell of success." That Ozzy, he's quite a card, isn't he?

Dedication's what you breed...

...if you wanna be a record-breaker!

Some people have too much time on their hands. There are many dog-related world records that are completely normal and non-threatening. For instance, the largest litter of puppies is 24, all born in 2004 to Tia, a Mastiff in Cambridgeshire. Similarly, the tallest dog is Gibson, a Great Dane who lives in California and is 107 centimetres tall. Likewise, the smallest living dog in length is just six inches long and is a Chihuahua called Heaven Sent Brandy who lives in Florida.

So far, so good. However, the very fact that there is a world record for the highest jump cleared by a dog is mildly bizarre.

For the record, it was a 167.6 centimetre jump achieved by a Greyhound called Cinderella May a Holly Grey who lives in Florida. (What is it with all these record-breaking dogs with ridiculous names in Florida?)

Moving from the mildly bizarre to the downright terrifying, have you ever found yourself unable to sleep through wondering what is the fastest time in which a dog has unwound a non-electric window? Us neither, but it is 11.34 seconds and was achieved by Striker, a Border Collie whose owners desperately need to find a new way to pass those long winter months.

The big ban

Hunting with dogs is outlawed

In 1979, Labour first promised to try and ban hunting with dogs. Well, in 2004 they finally managed it. Never in a hurry to get anything done, that red lot, are they? In the end, the Commons speaker had to invoke the Parliament Act to force through the legislation after the big posh sods in the House of Lords repeatedly blocked it. Well, they would, wouldn't they?

Anyway, the legislation banned fox-hunting, deer-hunting and hare-coursing with dogs. Conservative MP James Gray warned that the legislation sent a hidden message to the countryside, which read: "Cry havoc and let loose the dogs

of war." Silly man, it was the opposite of that message that was sent out!

That said, the posh people who loved hunting went absolutely potty. They stormed the House of Commons, chanting: "But we rule the world, we're big posh sods! How dare you do anything that we disagree with, you common-as-muck yobs!" OK, they didn't quite chant that, but you get the idea.

Everyone had their say on this issue, apart from the dogs. Even though this legislation left a lot of dogs with a lot of time on their paws, they remained as dignified and lovely as ever while human beings on all sides made complete arses of themselves.

The "IT" dog
Paris Hilton's Tinkerbell!

Dogs are definitely multi-talented animals, as we've firmly established throughout this book. But Tinkerbell Hilton is especially talented – she is an author! The teacup Chihuahua belonging to socialite Paris Hilton, in 2004, Tinkerbell published *The Tinkerbell Hilton Diaries*.

And there was plenty for Tinkerbell to write about. She has attended numerous parties, events and gatherings with her owner Paris, has appeared in the TV show *The Simple Life* and even went missing for six days when Paris's apartment was burgled.

What an eventful and purposeful life Tinkerbell has had – which proves that the adage that a dog is like its owner is not always true!

As we've seen, dogs regularly popped up in literature throughout the nineteenth and twentieth centuries. Happily enough, the twenty-first century shows little sign of this trend abating. The *Harry Potter* series features Fluffy, a three-headed guard dog which Hagrid bought off some Greek bloke down the pub. We've all done that. *The Curious Incident of the Dog in the Night-Time* by Mark Haddon is a remarkable tale of a boy with Asperger's Syndrome investigating the death of his neighbour's dog.

Meanwhile, over in Australia, the Louis de Bernières novel *Red Dog* has become a cult hit. It isn't the tale of some sinister left-wing dog; instead it tells the story of an enormously popular dog from Western Australia. Red Dog was a lovable Kelpie who travelled around Western Australia befriending families before heading off – often hitching a ride – to find a new family, often to return to say hi a few years later! De Bernières travelled around the region interviewing people who had come across the little dog and the result is a book that will make you literally weep with joy.

Best of breed: Whippets
Northern cross

Now then, now then: what's all this fuss and bother about Whippets? In 1800s, rabbit coursing were right popular in t'north of England. Oh aye, it were all t'rage back then. Originally, like, Terriers were used to chase rabbits, but then some good northern folk crossed the Italian Greyhound with the coursing Terriers and were right pleased with the result – the Whippet!

And little wonder: not only did the Whippet catch loads of rabbits, it was also cheaper to feed and house than the Greyhound. At the weekends, Whippets would provide entertainment when their owners

raced them against each other.

Quiet and gentle dogs, Whippets are very active and playful but also like to curl up and have a good sleep. They are trusting and friendly, so best not to invest in one if you are after a guard dog.

Down the years, the Whippet name has been adopted for cars and cookies, but you can keep your motors and your biscuits – if you want a right good friend, you can't do much better than a Whippet dog. Oh aye, southern people are so unfriendly. Why don't more folk just talk to each other nowadays. I'll tell you something (continued on page 687).

Rescue me!

Holly is the heroine

Holly, a three-year-old black Labrador from Lincolnshire, was honoured for her role in finding victims of the 2005 earthquake in Pakistan. Holly is on standby 365 days of the year for search and rescue operations. When the call came from south Asia, she went to Pakistan and worked 20 hours a day in extremely hot conditions without once complaining. She proved invaluable and located several people in collapsed buildings, and they were hauled to safety.

More than 73,000 people perished in the tragedy, but thanks to the efforts of Holly and other dogs, a number of lives were saved. What heroic little darlings they are.

The heroes of Ground Zero

Dogs join the paw on terror

When terrorists attacked America on September 11, 2001, our four-legged friends were immediately thrown into action. Dorado was the guide dog for New York resident Omar Eduardo Rivera and the pair found themselves on the 75th floor of the North Tower of the World Trade Center when it was hit. Despairing of any chance of escape for himself, Mr Rivera unleashed his dog, so that it might escape. Instead Dorado insisted on guiding his owner to safety. It took over an hour for Dorado to lead his owner down the 75 floors, but they managed to escape the World Trade Center minutes before the tower collapsed.

In the aftermath of the attacks, 350 search and rescue dogs were sent to Ground Zero and they managed to locate survivors in the rubble. Not that all dogs were there to search – some were taken along as therapy dogs to help boost the spirits of the rescue workers. Many of these workers insist the dogs were vital in helping them open up emotionally.

Less happy is the tale of Sirius, the bomb-sniffing dog who died in his kennel underneath the World Trade Center when the towers collapsed. This page is dedicated to him.

Best of breed: Labradors

Find and retrieve

They say you should leave the best until last. Well, we're not saying that Labradors are the best dog breed but they are certainly the most popular and high-profile of breeds in Britain and America. Whether it is through their courageous and loyal work as guide dogs or sniffer dogs, their appearances in numerous films including *The Shop on the High Street* and *The Incredible Journey*, Labradors have really contributed to the world.

However, what they have contributed most is, of course, lots of love. Originating in Great Britain during the 1800s, the Labrador Retriever is a loving, lovable and gregarious dog. They

are waterproof and used to retrieve the cork floats of fishing nets and swim them ashore for their masters in Canada in the olden days.

More recently they have become popular pets for families across the world. They live up to 13 years and have very friendly and gentle natures and get along wonderfully with children. If you throw a ball for them, they will run after it and bring it straight back to you every time. Which is why they are known as Labrador Retrievers. Pretty clever, huh?

99 Nintendogs
The computer canines!

All the talk of dogs throughout these pages may have made you keen to own one if you don't already. However, sometimes in life we are not allowed to get a dog because of nasty parents, partners or landlords.

While recognizing that the sort of person who prevents anyone from enjoying the fun of dog ownership is clearly a piece of scum, we would like to offer a compromise – the virtual dog! Oh yes, in these times when you can have a virtual version of virtually anything, it is now possible to own your very own computer dog!

Taking the lead from the Tamagotchi craze, the Nintendog offers you all the joys and tribulations of dog ownership via your computer. So that means you get the fun of owning a dog without any real carpets getting soiled and without you having to take anything on a walk in real rain.

While some purist dog owners may balk at this trend, the benefit is that it teaches youngsters exactly what dog ownership entails before they actually get a real dog. It does, one could almost add, show them all the joys of throwing a stick for a dog, only via their joysticks! Boom boom!

If you really love your dog, it is a huge heartbreak when it passes away to the great kennel in the sky. However, you might pretty soon be able to clone yourself a new version of your favourite pet! In August 2005, South Korean scientists unveiled the first cloned dog. The Afghan Hound was created by scientists at the Seoul National University (SNU) who named it Snuppy, which is a combination of "SNU" and "puppy". See what they've done there? Hilarious, eh?

Although other animals had already been cloned – including sheep, cats and rats – the successful cloning of a dog was a particular breakthrough as dogs are especially difficult to clone. Indeed, the scientists had to try 1,000 embryo transfers before they got lucky with Snuppy.

This all raises ethical dilemmas and a spokesman for the Kennel Club said it could "open up a whole new can of worms". Blimey? Are worms involved? No wonder there is such controversy surrounding this issue!

The end of the walk

Humble heroic hounds

Much like a good walk in the park with an excitable dog, the telling of the history of this glorious animal has been so eventful and energetic that we haven't had time to "paws" for reflection. However, now that we've got home, taken the leash off this book and allowed it to shake itself dry on the doormat, it's time to put our feet up and indulge in a bit of conclusive canine context.

Since they first came into contact with mankind, dogs have proved to be the most loyal, brave and generous of companions to the human race. From their courageous efforts in war and disaster zones, to search and rescue dogs sniffing out stranded humans and guide dogs helping the blind to live more normal

lives, there are few more humbling heroes than the hound.

Of course, everyday dogs are heroes, too. They say a dog is a man's best friend, but they're so much more than that. They are a full and loved member of families around the world. They make us laugh with their funny games, shower us with love and affection, cuddle up to us when we're sad and quite rightly scream at the postman when he brings us bills. How can we ever repay them for the happiness they bring us?

They are, of course, for life, not just for Christmas and we wouldn't have it any other way. Dogs, eh? Aren't they just the best?